FLORENTINE DRAWINGS

This volume, edited by ANDRÉ
GLOECKNER is one of the HY-
PERION Drawing Series and was
first published in nineteen hun-
dred and fifty by the Hyperion
Press. Printed by MOUTON & CO.
bound by H. VAN RIJMENAM,
The Hague

ANDRÉ CHASTEL, 1912 –

FLORENTINE DRAWINGS

XIV-XVII CENTURIES

Translated from French by Rosamund Frost

published by

THE HYPERION PRESS
New York . Paris . London

distributed by

THE MACMILLAN COMPANY
New York

Fotofacsimiles by Giraudon, Anderson, Alinari, Archives Photographiques,
British Museum, London, Metropolitan Museum, New York
Ancient map from the Bibliothèque Nationale, Paris

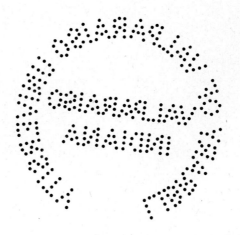

FLORENTINE DRAWINGS

THE first history of Italian art was published exactly four centuries ago by Vasari. It proclaimed the glory of Florence, even though the Tuscan Renaissance attained full stature only after his death. Several years after the appearance of his famous volume of *The Lives of the Most Eminent Painters, Sculptors and Architects,* Vasari decorated the halls of the Palazzo Vecchio with heroic historical frescoes and also built the long portico of the Uffizi to house the Grand Duchy's official business. The inheritance of this great day resulted in a bad painter, a mediocre architect, but a remarkable historian.

One of Vasari's most conspicuous traits was his interest in drawing. Ancestor of today's serious collectors, he compiled a group of albums planned to accompany the second edition of his *Lives*, saw to the mounting of the plates, and personally drew in their frames. Dispersed in the seventeenth century, fragments of these treasures reappear in the cabinet of Louis XIV and the Mariette collection. Today many are at the Louvre, though certain leaves ended up at the Uffizi. Beyond doubt, some of the drawings reproduced here passed through Vasari's hands. For there is a significant relationship between the cult of Florence, which the old "antiquarian" bequeathed to all his followers (including Ruskin and Berenson), and Vasari's insistence upon the history and even the theory of drawing.

When Vasari wrote: "drawing is the father of our three arts, architecture, sculpture and painting," he reiterated what is most self-evident and valuable in the long Florentine tradition. Drawing is like the inner principle of artistic activity, alone establishing a bond between all plastic arts. In this sense, Ghiberti termed it "foundation and theory". Half a century earlier, Leonardo endowed drawing with

5

the same philosophic virtues. Nor must we think of it as a hollow formula, a "device" ceremoniously conceived for the inaugural sessions of the Academy of Design, the first of their kind, of which the Grand Dukes of Tuscany were to become patrons. Think rather of the sheaves of drawings left by Michelangelo and Leonardo; of opening Vasari's treasures to extract one of those leaves on which one perceives the profile of a column, a study of hands destined to live in bronze, a notation concerning a high-light on drapery—all these juxtaposed at random and yet breathing the same spirit, delineated with a sharpness which endows a commonplace term with ultimate values. Here an outline echoes a piece of architecture; the reflections on a somber face of polished bronze are graphically analyzed—though the statue may not exist; a soaring church spire is noted with as much liveliness as a horse and rider. It was not merely a question of agility which made the Florentine artist carry all graphic expression to a point never again to be equalled in such variety and inventiveness. The insistence upon drawing as the secret main-spring of art suggests a certainty, a confidence in the realm of pure form rarely given its due.

Never was art theory more bravely intellectual. Like a product of the mind, the purely manual work of draftsmen was endowed with high spiritual significance. It is hard to decide which counted for most: the symbolism prized by the studios or the Platonism of the Humanists. Drawing emanated from an inner attitude which, so to speak, interrogated the subject then abandoned it for art's sake, so that the finished product might be truly "the visible expression of an inner idea *(concetto)* of the soul". In that instant between the glance at the model, the pressure of the hand on the paper—an instant that could pass like lightning or suspend judgment for hours—sensitivity stirred, intelligence spoke, the truth of art was challenged. This, for the initiates, was *the* artistic moment, sufficient in itself to establish the universal significance of drawing and set the standard of its integrity.

It has been suggested that practical distinctions should be made in regard to stages of execution, in order to facilitate the classification of certain basic types among the drawings we know. After the first *pensiero*, or sketch—a plan of organization "barely touched or lightly traced by the pen"—comes the *study* of details, exact and analytic, a preparation for the final, focussed *disegno*, which could serve as a model or solicit a client. This procedure illustrates the generally methodical approach of the Florentines. Such strict categorizing, however, is apt to be associated with hard-working, serious practitioners such as Ghirlandaio who were correspondingly short on genius.

Right from the start, Florentine drawing can be defined as a collection of outlines describing space and light on a piece of paper endowed with imaginary depth. A certain page of sketches, which Vasari surrounded by a "Gothic" frame and surmounted with a portrait of Cimabue, represents little figures and tight groups which at first glance might recall certain compositions dated around 1300. But the fine, broken pen-line which serves to indicate faces and hair, the long parallel strokes which render the folds of togas and the shadows, appear only at the beginning of the fifteenth century. We re-find them on a leaf whereon Ghiberti analyzed a silhouette for the Baptistery doors. This pseudo-Cimabue is perhaps the copy of an ancient work, but executed a century later, realistically, by Spinello Aretino. The pen technique is half scribbled. It claws at the forms while rounding them in, plastically. The opposite procedure is wash on colored paper, high-lighted by Chinese white. We have two magnificent examples of this technique in *The Presentation of the Virgin* by Taddeo Gaddi (regardless of whether this drawing was made before or after the Santa Croce fresco), and in the studies of Lorenzo Monaca. The luminous whites supply accent, even color. Underlying every stroke, the somber background suggests a nocturnal universe, mineral and glistening, whose fantastic poetry supports the romantic concept that faith will move mountains.

These two manners of evoking form, and the two types of result—volume built out of hatchings or melted in chiaroscuro—were progressively enriched by the virtuosity of the expanding fifteenth century. We find the first manner in the aggressive sketches of Pollaiuolo and in the notations of Leonardo, where the pen works with unprecedented freedom at a moment before cross hatching had transformed its intuitions into an analytical process. The second, chiaroscuro manner is all flexibility. In the astonishing *Head of a Monk*, attributed to Fra Angelico, but which is more probably a portrait (of the Blessed One?), by Benozzo Gozzoli, the economy of means afforded by alternate touches of white on a blue background is equalled only by the compulsion of the total effect. Filippo

7

Lippi, and after him his son Filippino, also experimented with this metamorphosis of forms swimming in blue and white chiaroscuro—a dream world which burnishes faces and immobilizes folds, turning ordinary cloth into silk.

But the main technical points are these : the play of hatchings to bring out dark on light, and the chiaroscuro technique which establishes high-lights on dark, playing up their animation and progressive sharpness (a great preoccupation in the Florentine studios), propounding that simple and disconcerting marvel of art, the contemplation of pure line. When Leonardo wrote, after Alberti and Piero della Francesca, "one must render the outlines of objects and their inflections with utmost care", he expressed a principle so obviously self-evident that it would hardly pass as even pseudo-technical advice. But such were the refinements that flourished in the "subtle air" of Florence that what appear to us banalities were approached as problems. What would seem easier, after all, than to enclose the object in an outline and, within this outline, suggest by a light shading *(sfumato)* the modeling that brings the form to life? This trivial injunction, however, goes back to Vitrivius; and it is this obvious process which the greatest Florentines conceived of as most mysterious and difficult. To Paolo Uccello, a few of whose striking drawings are known to us; to that individualist goldsmith Verrocchio who begat Leonardo; to the over-seductive Botticelli; to Michelangelo; to the successor Fra Bartolommeo and to the voluptuous, disturbing Pontormo, Florentine drawing represents a series of painstaking, refined, tender speculations on the beauty of line, its basic conventions, its alternately musical and structural overtones, its triumph and dissolution.

For a long period there has existed a type of art instruction in the western world which consists of reproducing in the most elegant possible calligraphy certain models, or *exemplars*, which became the caracteristic abbreviation of objects of interest. Once initiated into this kind of writing, any artist working around 1400 —say Cennino Cennini—could complete the drawing in the same spirit. (It was this very outline, regular, closed as a circle, devoid of depth as of atmosphere, of which the Florentines suddenly tired when the example of certain exacting masters of style introduced a new tension into art.) The tradition called for no more than a small hieroglyph, thin and artificial, on the pale surface of the paper. Its geometric and musical overtones (they are one); its endless counterpoint between threading line and hard margin attempt to interpret the true reality, rediscover the intangible, the moving aspects concealed under the banality of appearance. Florentines working in the taste of their time were stimulated in turn by love of geometric beauty (which, to the masters of 1430, was the supreme solution), by interest in motion as it reacted to an explosive stimulus, and finally by the seductive sweetness of the esthete and the neurotic.

Their tools perfected themselves and completed one another. The pen was ideal for the "naturalists", who prized a rough line and jagged forms. The "esthetes" formed under the influence of Verrocchio, Botticelli and Leonardo, used the silver-point, which produces a line as stinging as a wound and permits of an elaborate, refined modeling. This line in itself has a double function. When it is hard, it delimits; when it vibrates it suggests the enclosing atmosphere often more power-fully than the volume enclosed. Dry or humid air, the tremulous motion of hair or of cloth in impalpable space, all are noted on paper. Contrasts of wash on a dark ground seem almost too coarse for these nuances as the *sfumato* searches out the transparencies of the metal point. This is the moment when the chalk reveals its potentialities. Its vocabulary is rich, ranging from an almost furtive brushing on grey or salmon paper, to a grinding in with the full force of the wrist. More than their predecessors, Ghirlandaio and Luca Signorelli made general use of black chalk, *pietra nera*, the mineral ancestor of the pencil. Leonardo was the first to employ sanguine with its warm high-lights, a medium which Michelangelo defend-ed vigorously during the Sistine Chapel period. All these techniques are combined with incomparable richness of effect which transforms the humble drawing into a masterpiece: in short, the intellectual distillation of a style. Botticelli's superb *Abundance,* for instance, rehearses all these refinements : whatever is most delicate in the way of outline, surrounding space and modeling is rendered by the simul-taneous play of a fine pen point, a silverpoint, and white and black chalk synthe-sized into a masterpiece of poetic power.

Thus, thanks to drawing, a kind of second reality is born, more germane to the inner experiences of everyday life than superior to it, geared to the delights of esthetic contemplation. Filippino Lippi, many of whose pen and black chalk drawings have come down to us, proves that, even in his most successful works, dependence on these processes does not necessarily compensate for instability of inspiration. Like Piero di Cosimo, he is something of an unfulfilled Leonardo. As for this master himself, his drawings embody the whole complex of the physical world, animal life and its torments, the soul and its silences. In each successive line, alternately strong, broken, fluid or suppressed, Leonardo relentlessly studies the relationships between surrounding space and the surface of the object. Fine silverpoint hatchings conjure up smooth, rounded, radiant faces. A light wash, with high-lights, molds the fall of a drapery. A hundred times, the Florentine chalks evoke the wearied faces of the Apostles at the Last Supper; the monstrous grimaces of a human bestiary; and, in the late years, tempests, convulsions of air and water, catastrophies of nature. On the same piece of paper we may find a carefully-penned castle or a noble, moving physiognomy. The powdery surface, red with sanguine, black with chalk, still permits regular hatchings and the vigorous use of long lines which either attenuate form, (creating at times violent rhythms), or follow the contours of the modeling. The pen is sent on all kinds of cursive errands. It comes into its own in what are conventionally called the scientific drawings of Leonardo—studies of the vegetable world made with the analytical power of an engraver, outlines of dragons, horses, flayed men, gaping anatomies—in which the pen seems to wrench the last quiver out of the muscles. Thus drawing becomes the ideal instrument of knowledge, indispensable to the mind when it comes to transubstantiating what nature offers and conceals.

This overweening absorption with form, satisfiable only by the passionate exercise of drawing, is directed by Michelangelo upon the subject nearest at hand —his fellow-being—and practised less as a fine art than as plastic discipline. Michelangelo perfects the pen outline by the methodic use of cross-hatching and the play of tone to bring out relief. A bent torso, a raised shoulder hold as much variety for him as a landscape. Outline cuts sharply against these slopes and valleys; the hatched shadow competes with the high-light, energy broods in enormous panoramas of muscles. The total effect suggests a state of the soul. This was especially true toward the end of Michelangelo's days, when the aging artist admitted to Christian despair. His drawing becomes transformed. The outlines are lost; individual anatomy yields to mass effects; rubbing evokes on the paper the wan light of dramatic crucifixions.

After Michelangelo and Leonardo, drawing began to lose its usefulness to the sculptor and painter. Already with Fra Bartolommeo (the young artist whom Savonarola persuaded to become a monk), who once ranked with the big names, one feels the Florentine discipline and style weakening. This was evident either in disintegration of forms (which at this point needed the example of Raphael to degenerate into preciosity), or in exaggerated dynamism, interpreted in black chalk as heavy, summary masses. Since the sixteenth century, typically Umbrian taste for prettiness, built on the suggestive chiaroscuro of Leonardo, had anticipated the eddies and affectations which little by little eclipsed Florentine drawing.

But a new interpretation of the world came into being with the brilliant, unequal Andrea del Sarto, whose adept and often purist sketches in sanguine and black chalk attempt, by sheer grace, to escape from the overwhelming influence of Michelangelo. This independence is achieved by the astonishing Pontormo, many of whose sketches exist, and who remains the last of the great Florentine draftsmen. He betrays a sensitivity less controlled than Leonardo's. His specialty was a personal view of stock characters that a long line of artists had depicted before him. Drawn by him, Michelangelo's athletes become timid or immodest youths caught in a net of invisible, melodious lines. One sees his tall peasant women walk, and merge with uneasy groups. But the real subjects of these leaves are heat, cold, vague epidermal disquietudes. Over such compositions there floats a hypersensitive, troubled spirit, which would have astonished Vasari; a faint, voluptuous shiver which the descendants of Florentine Mannerism continued to re-echo until the seventeenth century—a final admission of the need for easier pleasures too long restrained by the demands of the intellect. This it is which, in retrospect, explains certain caprices of the quattrocento: the over-refined modeling of Verrocchio or Lorenzo di Credi, and even, possibly, the linear marvels of Botticelli.   ANDRÉ CHASTEL

BIBLIOGRAPHY

G. VASARI, *Le Vite dei piu eccelenti pittori, scultori ed architetti,* Ital. ed., G. Milanesi, Florence 1878, Vol. I *Vasari on Technique,* translated by L. S. Maclehose, introduction by G. Baldwin Brown, London, 1907.

J. MEDER, *Die Handzeichnung, ihre technik und Entwicklung,* Vol. II, Vienna, 1923.

H. S. EDE, *Florentine Drawings of the Renaissance,* London, 1926.

E. PANOFSKY, *Das erste Blatt aus dem "Libro" Giorgio Vasaris,* from "Städel-Jahrbuch", Frankfort-am-Main, VI, 1930.

O. KURZ, *Giorgio Vasari's "Libro dei Disegni",* from "Old Master Drawings", XII, 1937 Nos. 45 (June) and 47 (December).

B. DEGENHARDT, *Zur Graphologie der Handzeichnung,* from "Kunstgeschichtliches Jahrbuch der Biblioteca Hertziana", I, 1937, corrected in accordance with the observations of C. L. Ragghienti, Sul Metodo nello Studio dei Disegni, from the volume Commenti di Critica d'Arte, Bari, 1946.

B. BERENSON, *The Drawings of the Florentine Painters,* 3 vols., Chicago, 1938.

CH. DE TOLNAY, *History and Technique of Old Master Drawings,* New York, 1943.

P. LAVALLÉE, *Les Techniques du dessin,* 2nd edition, Paris, 1949.

FRA ANGELICO   1387-1455

Guido di Pietro Angelico, ecclesiastically called Fra Angelico da Fiesole, later beatified by the Church, was born near Vicchio in the Mugello. In 1407 he entered the Dominican monastery of Fiesole. In 1409, fleeing the aftermath of a religious schism, the monks of Fiesole fled to Foligno, returning only in 1418. This prolonged contact with the gentle mysticism of Umbria probably influenced the young monk. The paintings of his first period, up till 1430, derive from miniatures and are executed in a combination of the Giottesque and Sienese traditions. They comprise: the Madonnas of Parma and San Marco in Florence; *Christ in Glory* at the National Gallery, London; *The Annunciation* and *The Adoration of the Magi* of the San Marco Museum. The influence of Gentil Bellini is evident in *The Adoration of the Magi* and the *Last Judgment* of the San Marco Museum. However, from 1430 on perhaps and even, according to R. Longhi, from 1425 which would include the *Madonna of the Angels* of the Cook Collection, Richmond), there appear experiments in perspective and volume plus an expression of spatial values which proclaim the influence of Masaccio, namely in the Louvre *Coronation of the Virgin*; the *Descent from the Cross* of San Marco; and the Perouse triptych. In 1436, the Fiesole Dominicans established themselves in Florence proper in the Convent of San Marco, which Michelozzi undertook to reconstruct in 1437. Between 1439 and 1455, Fra Angelico decorated this monastery with an admirable group of frescoes which represent the summit of Christian art. Towards 1445, he was called to Rome to decorate for the Vatican and Pope Nicholas V the chapel of St. Stephen and St. Laurence. This was for him a period of intense activity. He had numerous pupils, among them Baldovinetti and Benozzo Gozzoli. Named Prior of the monastery in 1451, he died in Rome four years later.

FRA BARTOLOMMEO   1472-1517

Bartolommeo di Paolo, called Baccio della Porta, was born in Florence. In 1485, he became a Rosselli apprentice and a warm friend of Mariotto Albertinelli. Together they opened a studio in 1492. The violent sermons of Savonarola, in particular those which stigmatized profane and voluptuous painting, preyed on his mind and in his enthusiasm he decided to burn all his secular works prior to 1496. In 1497, he undertook *The Last Judgment* for the cemetery of Santa Maria Nuova. In 1500, he entered the Domincan monastery of Prato as a novice. Returning to Florence in 1501, he spent his remaining life at San Marco. An acquaintance with Raphael in 1507 was for him a revelation, and several years later Fra Bartolommeo rejoined him in Rome. Relics of this visit are *The Eternal Adored by Sts. Madeleine and Catherine* (1509) and the big composition, *Virgin and Saints,* 1512 (Ufizzi). Michelangelo, who had just completed the Sistine Chapel, in turn exercised so profound an influence on Fra Bartolommeo that he proposed to give up painting. He changed his mind on the latter but thereafter went in for declamatory compositions such as *Christ Arisen,* 1516 (Pitti).

BENOZZO GOZZOLI   1420-1498

Benozzo di Sandro di Lese was born in Florence in 1420. Favorite pupil and collaborator of Fra Angelico, both in San Marco and in Rome, he attempted to combine the suavity of the latter with the lyric pictorialism of Gentile da Fabriano to form a facile, flowery art. He painted several large fresco cycles, *The Life of St. Francis* at San Francesco di Montefalco; and *The Journey of the Magi* for the chapel of the Palazzo Medici, in which numerous contemporaries are represented in an unreal landscape which presents both Oriental and Tuscan elements. In 1463, he embarked upon the important cycle of *The Life of St. Augustin* in San Gimigniano, then (1468-84) executed the Old Testament cycle for the Campo Santo in Pisa, where he betrays beneath his narrative ease a certain influence of Fra Filippo Lippi and Botticelli.

BOTTICELLI   1444?-1510

Allessandro, or Sandro, Botticelli was born in Florence between 1444 and '45. He began as a goldsmith apprentice, then entered the atelier of Fra Filippo Lippi, the great painter of the period. In the early stages, he was subjected equally to the influences of Verrocchio and Pollaiuolo in whose studios he worked, and soon became a painter of Madonnas which were much admired for the grace of his composition. In 1481, he went to Rome to paint three of the Sistine Chapel frescoes : *Christ Tempted by Demons, Moses and the Daughters of Jethro, The Sacrifice of the Children of Aaron.* He also executed the two "wedding" frescoes of the Villa Lemmi, since removed to the Louvre. Shortly after his trip to Rome, he painted the celebrated secular pictures, *Alle-*

gory of Spring, The Birth of Venus, Pallas and the Centaur (Ufizzi). The portraits which he executed in fairly large number have a curious character of dreamy melancholy. His art grew increasingly linear and allusive. Converted by the preachings of Savonarola, he burned his pagan works in 1495 and thereafter gave himself up with great fervor to religious paintings (*The Entombment,* Milan and Munich), and, later, *The Nativity* (National Gallery, London). He made a series of drawings as illustrations for *The Divine Comedy* which rank among the finest graphic transeriptions of this epic.

CIGOLI   1559-1613

Lodovico Cardi, called Cigoli, is, along with Cristofano Allori, one of the last of the Tuscan Mannerists. His is a court art, declamatory and official, of an artificial sweetness but sometimes showing a certain delicacy.

PIERO DI COSIMO   1462-1521

From his real appellation of Piero di Lorenzo, the artist adopted the first name of Cosimo Roselli, his master. In 1481, he accompanied Rosselli to Rome and worked with him on the Sistine Chapel decorations, a large section of *The Crossing of the Red Sea* being attributed to him. Piero di Cosimo reacted to the successive influences of Verrocchio; of Botticelli in his portrait of Simonetta Vespucci (Chantilly Museum); of Lorenzo di Credi in his *Portrait of a Woman* (Galleria Corsini, Rome) and finally of Leonardo. To be included also are certain

Flemish painters well known in Florence since the appearance (toward 1482) of Hugo van der Goes' Portinari Triptych. The most original part of his work resides, perhaps, in his *cassoni* panels ornamented, for the most part, with mythological subjects treated with charming humor and fantasy, such as *Mars and Venus* (Berlin), *Procris* (National Gallery), *The Legend of Perseus* (Berlin, Ufizzi) and *The Battle of the Centaurs and the Lapidae* (Richetts and Shannon Coll., London). These form a part of a series describing the story of primitive humanity (*Return from the Hunt,* Metropolitan Museum, New York) which combine acrid commentary with an already romantic feeling for landscape.

LORENZO DI CREDI   1459?-1537

His real name was Lorenzo d'Andrea d'Oderigo. Entered in Verrocchio's studio, he was a co-pupil of Perugino and Leonardo. Deep bonds of affection existed between him and his master, whose executor he became, the Pistoia retable, commissioned of Verrocchio being almost entirely from his hand. Under evident influence of Leonardo, he manifested a new interest in the atmosphere which envelops the landscape. But he soon developed a formula of which the best expressions are: the two *Madonnas,* one in Turin, the other in Mayence; *The Blessed* (Cleveland Art Museum); an *Annunciation* (Ufizzi); and a *Venus* which shows direct study of the naked model, being almost of the same stature as a similar composition of Botticelli.

ANDREA DEL SARTO   1486-1531

Andrea Vanucci, called del Sarto, was born in Florence in 1486. A pupil of Piero di Cosimo, gratuated in 1508, he worked first in collaboration with his friend Franciabigio showing considerable understanding of Leonardo's delicate *sfumato*. His first commissions were frescoes for the small cloister of the Annunziata in Florence: five compositions recapitulating the life of St. Philip Binazzi, to which he later added an *Adoration of the Magi* and a *Birth of the Virgin*. The *Annunciation* of the Pitti is of 1513, the Dresden *Marriage of St. Catherine* is probably of the same period. The following year he undertook for the convent of the barefoot Carmelites the *Life of St. John the Baptist,* a grisaille fresco. Of the year 1517 dates the *Madonna,* called *"of the Harpies"* notable for its accomplished composition and melting, tender color. Toward the end of his life, he painted two important works, *The Assumption,* of which the Pitti owns two variants, and the *Last Supper* from the Convent of San Salvi, inspired by Leonardo and of a rather cold classicism.

GHIBERTI   1378-1455

Lorenzo di Cione di Ser Buonaccorso, born in Florence in 1378, began as a goldsmith then, in 1403, was commissioned as the result of a celebrated competition to execute the second bronze door of the Baptistery. From 1418 to 1431, he collaborated with Brunelleschi in building the dome of the cathedral of Florence, and at the same time worked on its stained glass windows. His atelier received innumerable orders for chalices, jewelery and such. Like the whole of his art, his drawings are full of style and retain a Gothic rhythm even while producing Renaissance effects. His *Commentarii* present important testimony on both the theory and the aspect of quattrocento Florence.

GHIRLANDAIO 1449-1494?

Domencio di Tommaso, born in Florence, formed his art in the studio of Baldovinetti without retaining his master's incisive strength. On the contrary, Ghirlandaio represents a certain yielding to easy storytelling. His group pictures amply evoke wellknown figures of the local bourgeoisie. Working in collaboration with his brothers, David and Benedetto, he composed several large fresco cycles : in the Santa Fina Chapel in San Gimigniano (1475), in the Sistine Chapel in Rome and, above all, *The Life of St. Francis* frescoes in the Sassetti Chapel of Santa Trinitá in Florence (1485), as well as those in the choir of Santa Maria Novella. He strove for simple harmonies, well-ordered compositions, ample forms and gay colors. Michelangelo was his pupil.

GIOVANNI DA SAN GIOVANNI 1592-1636

Pupil of Matteo Rosselli, influenced by the Caracci, this Florentine of compositional ingenuity was one of the first Baroque decorators in Rome, among his works the choir representing *Four Crowned Saints* and, in Tuscany, paintings in the Badia of Fiesole.

FILIPPO LIPPI 1406?-1469

Fra Filippo Lippi was born in Florence at the beginning of the fifteenth century, entered a Carmelite monastery at an early age and became the protégé of Cosimo de' Medici, who took an indulgent attitude toward the escapades of the young monk. In 1437, working in the Convent of Prato, he eloped with a nun and by her had a son, Filippino, who in turn became a painter. The Humanist Pope Pius II relieved him of his vows and eventually the two delinquents were legally married. Filippo's special contribution was the introduction of a certain profane beauty into the traditional themes of religious art, including the truly feminine type of his Madonnas. In the beginning, he painted under the influence of Fra Angelico graceful pictures such as *The Annunciation* (Ufizzi). Toward 1440, his art took on a "modern" turn with *The Virgin and Saints* (Louvre) and *The Crowning of the Virgin* (Vatican, Ufizzi) which are enriched by a kind of luminous chairoscuro. The versions of *The Virgin Adoring the Child* are of a richness rare in Florentine art. Finally, in his frescoes for the Prato Cathedral executed after 1452, Filippo demonstrates a harmonious power of composition of which another example is the decoration of the cathedral of Spoleto, which was interrupted by his death.

FILIPPINO LIPPI 1457-1504

Born in Prato, the son of Filippo, Filippino, on his father's death was placed in charge of the latter's collaborator, Fra Diamante, who apprenticed him to Botticelli. In his first period, the influence of Filippo and Botticelli are particularly noticeable, as seen in *The Apparition of the Virgin to St. Bernard* (Badía, Florence). Invited by the Carmine monks to finish the incomplete frescoes of Masaccio, he conformed with ease to the latter's monumental grandeur in order to paint *The Story of St. Peter and St. Paul*. His *Apparition of the Virgin to St. Bernard* (1486) is celebrated. He accompanied Botticelli to Rome to help him in his work on the Sistine Chapel (1481-82) and became absorbed in the remains of Roman civilization, as witnessed by *The Story of St. Thomas Aquinas* in the Caraffa Chapel, Minerva, and the frescoes of *The Lives of Sts. Philip and John* executed toward the century's end for the Strozzi Chapel of Santa Maria Novella in Florence. In these animated and often bizarre compositions, certain Mannerist and pre-Baroque traits are evident. He is one of the Florentines of whom we have a major record in sketches and drawings.

MASACCIO   1401-1428

Tommaso di Giovanni, born at San Giovanni Valdarno, is the greatest name in Florentine painting after Giotto, whose "plastic" style he renewed, and preceding Michelangelo, whose dramatic intensity he foretold. Vasari's claim that he was a pupil of Masolino is hardly credible; undoubtedly the young painter collaborated with this facile but genuine master in the Brancacci Chapel of the Carmine in Florence, but the section of the frescoes which he can claim (*Adam and Eve, The Story of St. Peter*) shows that, from the first, his style was of a vigor, even an expressive violence which was entirely new. Masaccio was the friend of Donatello and of Brunelleschi whose exclamations of sorrow upon learning of the untimely death of the young artist in Rome is wellknown. Masaccio painted a *St. Anne* (Ufizzi), a retable (now

dispersed) for Pisa and worked on the frescoes of San Clemente in Rome.

MICHELANGELO   1475-1564

Michelangelo Buonarroti was born in Caprese in the province of the Casentino, of which his father was governor. As a young child, he worked with the sculptor Bertoldo and learned painting with Chirlandaio. At 15, he was noticed by Lorenzo il Magnifico, who drew him into his entourage. He went to Rome in 1496 and sculpted the *Drunken Bacchus, Cupid Kneeling* and his *Pietá*. Back in Florence, he extracted from an unused block of marble his gigantic *David* (1502), which won him glory. Upon the accession of Julius II, Michelangelo was called to Rome. There, having sketched the formidable tomb of the Popes which was destined to haunt him for the rest of his life and of which only the *Moses* and the *Slaves* remain, he devoted himself for four years to the decoration of the Sistine Chapel, whose richness of plastic invention left its mark on his whole century. Returning in 1520 to sculpture, Michelangelo embarked on the tomb of the Medicis in the new sacristy of San Lorenzo in Florence. Definitely established in Rome in 1534, the artist dedicated himself to the fiery *Last Judgment* of the Sistine Chapel. He worked on it for five years. His architectural career was hardly less important. With the dome of St. Peter's, whose first plans went back to Bramante, he found an edifice that measured up to him. He devoted his old age to it, creating a new type of architecture which, by the force of its impact and the importance of its masses, is the summit of

17

classic art. All these works were accompanied by admirable drawings in which Michelangelo has left a record of the measure of his genius for plastic analysis.

DOMENICO MICHELINO   1417-1491

The fresco in the Cathedral of Florence representing Dante before the three other worlds, dated 1465, is the only authenticated worked of this painter, who was a pupil of Fra Angelico and Baldovinetti.

POLLAIUOLO   1429-1498

Antonio di Jacopo Pollaiuolo began as a goldsmith apprentice in the workshop of his father. According to Vasari, he worked on the third bronze door of the Florentine Baptistery. In 1459, he set up his own goldsmith shop near the Ponte Vecchio in Florence. His fame as a sculptor was great and after 1490 he executed the bronze tombs of the two popes. Sixtus IV and Innocent VIII. Celebrated as a painter and designer, he was strongly influenced by Andrea del Castagno, his art attaining a kind of cruel power in the *Labors of Hercules* (toward 1460). In 1475, he painted the *Martyrdom of St. Sebastian* in the National Gallery, which soon became famous. His last known painting is *The Coronation of the Virgin* executed for the collegiate church of San Gimigniano. Like his sculpture, his painting shows a passion for the sharp, incisive line. His harsh, nervous style deeply influenced Botticelli and Signorelli.

PONTORMO   1495-1556

Jacopo Carucci, called Pontormo, was born in 1495 in the town of this name near Empoli, and was buried in Florence in 1556. He moved to Florence in 1507. According to Vasari, he was the pupil of Leonardo and Andrea del Sarto. But Piero di Cosimo was no less important in his development. Later, Michelangelo's accomplishments added certain overtones to an art already imbued with nervosity, in which we can even detect a trace of the Northern engravers such as Dürer. In this sense, he represents the last figure of the Florentine Renaissance and the first Mannerist. Along with his frescoes of *The Visitation* in the cloister of the Annunciata, one must cite above all the admirable lunette painted at Poggio a Caiano for the Villa Medici of which numerous studies and projects exist, also the *Deposition* of Santa Felicita, *The Martyrdom of St. Mauritius* (Ufizzi) and portraits of great brilliance and elegance, such as his studies of young boys in London and Milan.

ROSSO FIORENTINO   1495-1541

Giambattista di Jacopo, called Rosso, was, with Pontormo, the Florentine master of Mannerism. His art derives from the supple style of Andrea del Sarto but includes planar experiments (*The Deposition* of Volterra), an unreal and violently dramatic illumination *Marriage of the Virgin* and a taste for interlaced compositions and strong plastic effects derived from Michelangelo. It is in this complicated and often bizarre spirit that he decorated the Galerie François I at Fontainebleau.

FRANCESCO DE ROSSI, called CECCHINO
SALVIATI 1510-1563

Pupil of *Pontormo* and *Andrea del Sarto*, he decorated the audience hall of the Palazzo Vecchio with allegorical and historical frescoes, in the same academic spirit as his contemporary *Vasari*. Yet in his portraits, as well as in his composition pictures (Charity, Galleria di Ufizzi), *Salviati* possesses a style of such ease and limpidity that he numbers among the most remarkable of the mannerist Florentine painters.

LUCA SIGNORELLI   1441?-1523

Born in Cortona between Florence and Umbria, he was the pupil of Piero della Francesca, whom he assisted in the latter's Arezzo frescoes. Thereafter, he entered into the orbit of Pollaiuolo's dynamic art. Toward 1480, he frescoed the basilica of Loretto. Of this same period are the *Angels, Prophets* and *Apollo* of the great retable of Perouse and the celebrated, now destroyed, painting of *Pan* once of the Berlin Museum. In 1497, he painted in the convent of Monte Oliveto nine frescoes out of a series representing the life of St. Benedict which Sodoma was destined to complete. In 1499, he was called on to finish, in the new chapel of the Orvieto Cathedral, the frescoes begun by Fra Angelico. There he painted his masterpieces, *The Last Judgment* and the scenes of *The Apocalypse, Heaven* and *Hell*. In their expressive "ferocity", their richness of plastic invention, these frescoes are the direct forerunners of the Michelangelo of the Sistine Chapel.

ARETINO SPINELLO   1346?-1410

Born in Arezzo, he was a pupil of Agnolo Gaddi, and showed traces of Nardo's and Andrea di Cione's (Orcagna) style. He decorated the chapel of Pieve in Arezzo, finished an altar-piece for the church of San Ponziano in Lucca, painted various frescoes for the sacristy of San Miniato al Monte in Florence and the neighboring chapel of Antella around 1387 ("Story of Saint Catherine") and finally worked at the Camposanto in Pisa. He died in Arezzo. Spinello remained the last representative artist of value in the Giotto tradition. According to B. Berenson, a number of drawings among which some copies of old masterpieces are due to his hand, while some other drawings, after the Navicella of Giotto, are probably the work of his son, Parri Spinelli.

PAOLO UCCELLO   1397-1475

Paolo di Dono was born and died in Florence. According to Vasari, his nickname Uccello was a reference to his love of birds. In 1415, he entered the corporation of "Medici e Speciali", and in 1424 became a member of the Company of St. Luke. In 1425 he rewrote his will before leaving for Venice, where he lived until 1430, working as mosaicist in San Marco. Upon returning to Florence, he executed the frescoes for the cathedral and the cloister of San Marco of which some fragments have been recently brought to light. His training as a sculptor explains his passionate preoccupation with volume in painting. The Gothic cast which distinguishes

19

his first works was dissipated under the influence of Brunelleschi, Donatello and Masaccio. Among his principle works are: his monochrome frescoes in the Chiostro Verde of Santa Maria Novella, in which he devotes himself to the experiments in perspective which he passionately loved; the equestrian figure of *Condottiere John Hawkwood* in the interior of the Duomo; three battle panels painted for the Medici Palace which are currently at the Ufizzi, the Louvre and the National Gallery. In 1455 he executed for the Corpus Domini of Urbino a retable of which the predella remains a work in the Surrealist taste, as is the nocturnal Hunt in the Ashmolean at Oxford. Bathed in fantastic colors, his " abstractions " rank among the most remarkable works of the Florentine School.

VASARI   1511-1574

Giorgio Vasari, painter, architect and art historian, was closely associated with the intellectual and artistic movement of the sixteenth century. He frequented and served the great names of the day; he was the familiar of the best-known artists. His fame is based primarily on his monumental collection of biographies, *The Lives of the Most Eminent Painters, Sculptors and Architects* begun around 1542 at the request of Cardinal Farnese and first published in 1550. His early works were criticized by Andrea del Sarto and Michelangelo. In Rome he pursued his studies in the company of Francesco Salviati. In 1531, he established himself in Florence at the court of Duke Allessandro de' Medici then, when the latter was assassinated in 1537, he moved to Parma, where he

studied the art of Correggio, to Venice, where he became the friend of Pietro Aretino, to Bologna (*The Feast of St. Gregory*) and finally to Naples. In 1547 he completed the frescoes ordered by Cardinal Farnese for the chancellery in Rome. Aided by pupils, he worked in the Roman churches and at the Villa Giulia. Official prince of art, overwhelmed by orders, he composed immense frescoes with a rapidity and facility which are only too evident. He built the Ufizzi Palace, the secret cabinet of Francesco de' Medici, decorated halls of the Vatican and the Lateran and founded a Florentine drawing academy. He died after having undertaken to paint the dome of Santa Maria del Fiore.

LEONARD DE VINCI   1452-1519

A natural son of Ser Pietro, notary to the Signoría of Florence, who apprenticed him to Verrocchio, he learned both painting and sculpture. Gifted with an extraordinary combination of physical and intellectual qualities, he revealed himself from the first as a poet, a musician, a philosopher while at the same time devoting himself to all the sciences. *The Adoration of the Magi,* of which the incomplete sketch remains, and the *Madonna of the Rocks* are the earliest proofs of his utter originality. He left Florence in 1482 for Milan and the service of Lodovico il Moro. The duke employed him as palace decorator and organizer of fêtes, and commissioned him to make a statue of his father, Francesco Sforza. In 1498 he completed the *Last Supper* of Santa Maria delle Grazie. Returning to Florence in 1501, he painted *St. Anne,* then the cartoon for the never-realized fresco, *The Battle of the Angiari* — two works which drew the admiration of his time. The *Gioconda* is of similar date. He returned to Milan at the request of Charles d'Amboise and Juliano de' Medici. Raphael's jealousy precluded his taking part in the great works of the Vatican. In 1516, he went to Bologna, where he encountered Francois I. Invited to the Château of Cloux, near Amboise, he ended his days here. An inventor and engineer, constantly planning new scientific treatises, Leonardo is well known for his drawings which offer a variety and strange power possessed by no other artist.

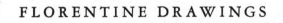

FLORENTINE DRAWINGS

Head of a Monk

BENOZZO GOZZOLI   Chantilly, Musée Condé

25

La Navicella

FLORENTINE SCHOOL XIVth CENTURY   Bayonne, Musée Bonnat

26   (attributed by B. BERENSON to PARRI SPINELLI)

Scenes From the Life of a Saint

ARETINO SPINELLO   Paris, Ecole des Beaux-Arts

27

La Navicella

FLORENTINE SCHOOL XIVth CENTURY   New York, Metropolitan Museum of Art

(attributed by B. BERENSON to PARRI SPINELLI)

28

Calling of *the Apostles*

Domenico di Michelino (?)   Paris, Musée du Louvre

PROPHAETA   DAVID

The Prophet David

FRA ANGELICO   London, British Museum
30

Profile of a Man

UCCELLO   Florence, Uffizi

Scenes From

Masaccio (after)

of Saints
Paris, Musée du Louvre

Sketch for Equestrian Statue of Sir John Hawkwood

Florence, Uffizi

St. Laurence

BENOZZO GOZZOLI   Windsor Castle, Royal Library

By gracious permission of H. M. the King   35

Female Saint

FILIPPO LIPPI   London, British Museum
36

Saint John

ROSSO FIORENTINO   Florence, Uffizi

Draperies

BENOZZO GOZZOLI

London, Harwood Collection

38

Five Studies for Executioners

Lorenzo Ghiberti   Albertina, Vienna

Study for Three Men, Two Seated and One Brandishing a Staff
Paris, Musée du Louvre
SCHOOL OF UCCELLO

A. POLLAIUOLO

Study for Tobias and The Angel
Paris, Musée du Louvre

Hercules and Hydra

A. POLLAIUOLO   London, British Museum

42

Two Students in Conversation

FILIPPINO LIPPI   Paris, Ecole des Beaux-Arts

43

Man Seated, Man Standing

FILIPPINO LIPPI

London, British Museum

44

Eva

A. POLLAIUOLO

Florence, Uffizi

45

Two Male Figures

FILIPPINO LIPPI   New York, Metropolitan Museum of Art
46

Nude Man

FILIPPINO LIPPI   London, British Museum

47

Cave at Side of Jagged Cliff in Romantic Wilderness

PIERO DI COSIMO

Florence, Uffizi

48

Landscape

FRA BARTOLOMMEO   Paris, Musée du Louvre

49

St. John the Baptist Standing

LORENZO DI CREDI   Paris, Musée du Louvre
50

Two Figures Illustrating Opening of 33rd Canto of Dante's Inferno

SIGNORELLI

London, British Museum

Studies of Draped Male Figure, Standing, and Head of a Man
SANDRO BOTTICELLI
Paris, Musée du Louvre

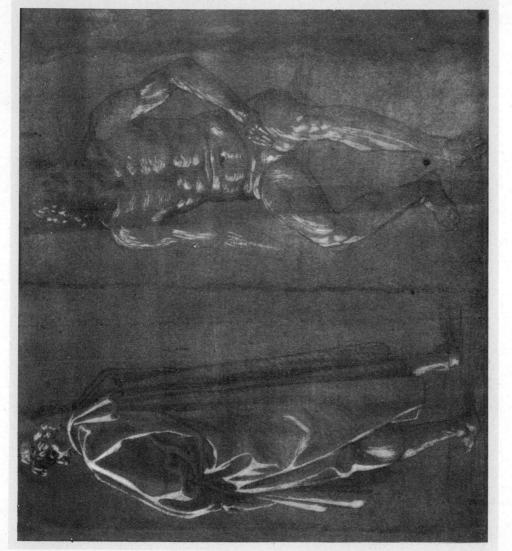

D. GHIRLANDAIO   *A Draped Figure and a Nude*   London, British Museum

Head of an Elderly Man

D. GHIRLANDAIO

London, British Museum

54

Profile of Youth With Lank Streaming Hair

D. GHIRLANDAIO

Paris, Musée du Louvre

Drawing to Illustrate Dante's Divina Comedia (Paradiso, Canto XX)
Berlin, Print room
SANDRO BOTTICELLI

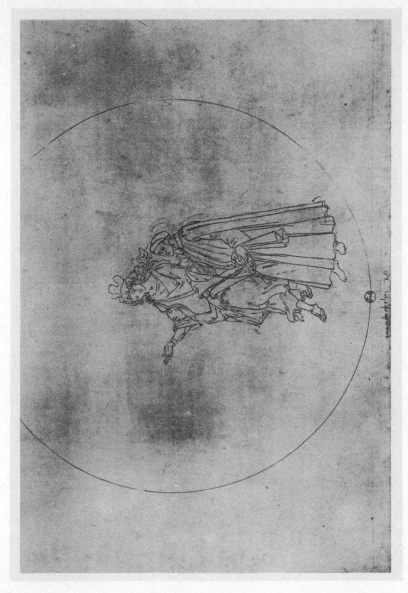

Drawing to Illustrate Dante's Divina Comedia (Paradiso, Canto XX)
Berlin, Print room
SANDRO BOTTICELLI

57

Drawing to Illustrate Dante's Divina Comedia (Paradiso, Canto I)
Berlin, Print room

SANDRO BOTTICELLI

Drawing to Illustrate Dante's Divina Comedia (Purgatory, Canto XXIII)
Berlin, Print room

SANDRO BOTTICELLI

59

Faith

SANDRO BOTTICELLI

London, British Museum

60

Abundance

SANDRO BOTTICELLI

London, British Museum

61

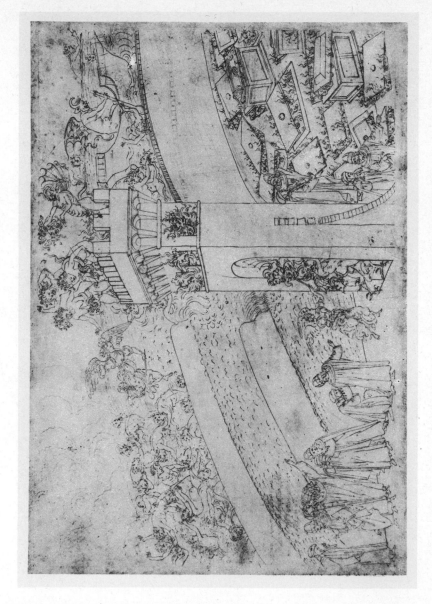

Drawing to Illustrate Dante's Divina Comedia *(Inferno, Canto IX)*
Rome, Vatican Library
SANDRO BOTTICELLI

Dead Christ in the Lap of His Mother, With Two Saints
Paris, Musée du Louvre

FILIPPINO LIPPI

Drawing to Illustrate Dante's I
SANDRO BOTTICELLI

64

...media *(Inferno, Canto XXXI)*
Berlin, Print room

Angel

Fra Bartolommeo   Vienna, Albertina

66

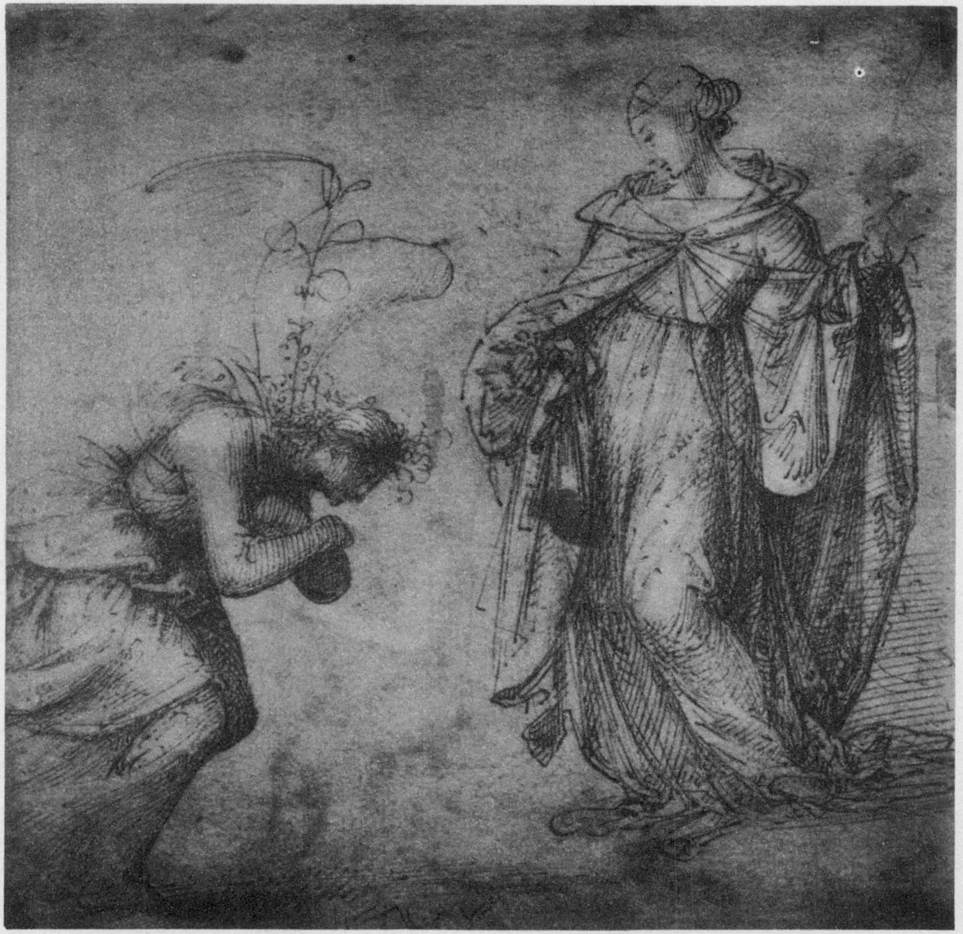

The Annunciation

FRA BARTOLOMMEO — Paris, Musée du Louvre

Venus On Pedestal and Women and Children Grouped Around Her
Florence, Uffizi

FRA BARTOLOMMEO

Fra Bartolommeo   Study for an Altar's Painting   Florence, Uffizi

Study for a Virgin's Coronation

Fra Bartolommeo

70

Paris, Musée du Louvre

Palm-Tree

Fra Bartolommeo   London, British Museum

Apollo

Florence, Uffizi

Bust of a Young Man

PONTORMO

Florence, Uffizi

73

Putto

PONTORMO   Florence, Uffizi
74

Men on Horseback

PONTORMO

Florence, Uffizi

75

PONTORMO · *Youthful Reclining Nude* · Florence, Uffizi

Study for Reclining Shepherdess   Florence, Uffizi

PONTORMO

Self-Portrait

LEONARDO DA VINCI

Turin, Royal Library

78

Study for the Head of St. Anne

<small>LEONARDO DA VINCI</small>   Windsor Castle, Royal Library

79

Landscape

LEONARDO DA VINCI

the Arno

Florence, Uffizi

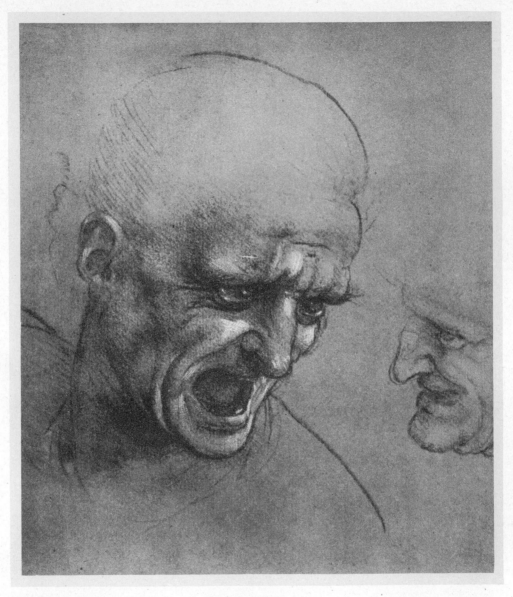

Heads of Warriors

LEONARDO DA VINCI

82

Budapest, Museum of Fine Arts

Antique Warrior

LEONARDO DA VINCI

London, British Museum

Leda and the Swan

Leonardo da Vinci   Haarlem, Coll. Franz Koenigs

84

Madonna with the Fruit-Plate

LEONARDO DA VINCI   Paris, Musée du Louvre

Studies for the Trivulzion Monument

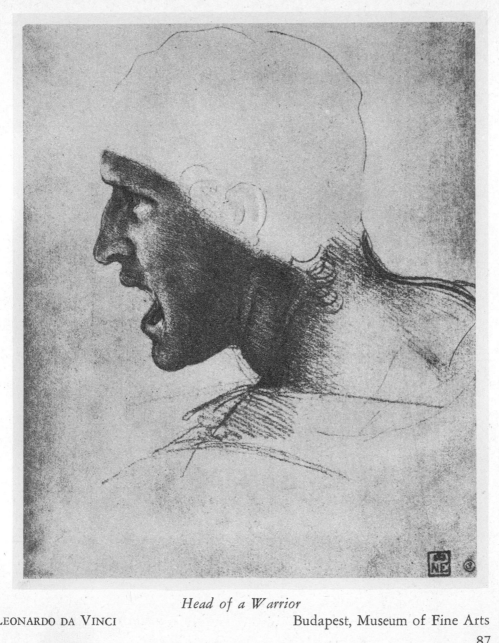

Head of a Warrior

Storm in the Alps

LEONARDO DA VINCI   Windsor Castle, Royal Library

88

Man on Horseback

Leonardo da Vinci

Florence, Uffizi

Study for Hands   Paris, Musée du Louvre

MICHELANGELO

Bust of a Woman

ANDREA DEL SARTO   Paris, Musée du Louvre

91

The Dead Christ

MICHELANGELO   Vienna, Albertina

92   (attributed by B. BERENSON to SEBASTIANO DEL PIOMBO)

Study for a Bather

MICHELANGELO London, British Museum

93

Study of Frightened Man Seen from the Back

SCHOOL OF MICHELANGELO   Paris, Musée du Louvre

94

ANDREA DEL SARTO

Study for Four Apostles

Florence, Uffizi

Two Men Wrestling

MICHELANGELO
96

Paris, Musée du Louvre

The Descent from the Cross

MICHELANGELO   Haarlem, Teyler Museum

97

Studies for the Libyan Sibyl

Seated Female Figure, Facing to the Left and Holding a Child in Her Out-Stretched Arms
MICHELANGELO   Paris, Musée du Louvre
(attributed by B. BERENSON to SEBASTIANO DEL PIOMBO)   99

Study for Christ Judging of Sistine Chapel

MICHELANGELO

Montpellier, Musée Fabre

100

Diane and Endymion

L. Cigoli

Florence, Uffizi

F. SALVIATI   *Spring*   Florence, Uffizi

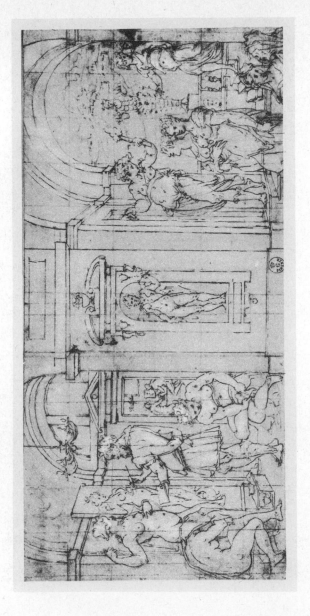

GIORGIO VASARI

Painting, Allegory

Florence, Uffizi

Three Men

<small>Florentine School xvith Century</small>   New York, Metropolitan Museum of Art

104

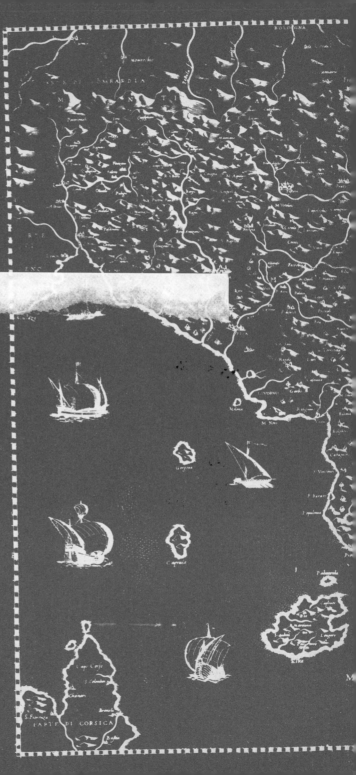

En candidi Lectores, elegantioris Italiæ partis, Tusciæ scilicet Topogra
phiam, æneis nostris formis excusam in hac Tabella vobis domus damus,
atque ita quidem absolute, ut nihil amplius in ea desideraturi reperiri, præter
tum quod, cum adiacentibus Vmbria, Æmilia, Lombardia, &
Liguriæ partibus ad unguem fuerit effigiata. In qua consti-
enda hæc nos præstare conati sumus, ut singu-
oppida, Montes, Flumina, Lacus, Portus, Insu-
ratu digna Littoribus maris Tusci adiacentia pa-
diligentissime describeremus. Quæ omnia ab his qui oculata
nobis cuncta retulerunt didicimus. Non Vos pigeat igitur optimi
Lectores hac Tabellam paulum oculos contemplari si germanam
& exactam Tusciæ descriptionem intelligere desideratis.

   Locorum distantiam sic inuenies

  Aperto Circino cape quæsita loci distantiam eamque ad line
    am hanc applica, mox lineola circum pedibus inclusa
      mensuresque secantes miliaria in decaboues, quod
        si distantia inuenta maior ipsa linea
          sit, per partes rem expedire opor
              tebit

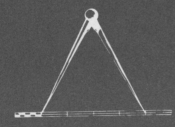